PROFITS FROM PASSION

TRANSFORMING YOUR LEISURE PURSUIT INTO A PROFITABLE VENTURE

BY

ROBERT T. AGUILAR

PROFITS FROM PASSION

Copyright © 2023 by Robert T. Aguilar

PROFITS FROM PASSION

TABLE OF CONTENT

INTRODUCTION 5

CHAPTER ONE 7

   ASSESSING THE VIABILITY OF YOUR HOBBY AS A BUSINESS 7

   DETERMINING IF THERE IS A MARKET DEMAND FOR YOUR HOBBY 7

   UNDERSTANDING YOUR POTENTIAL TARGET AUDIENCE AND COMPETITION 10

   EVALUATING YOUR SKILLS AND RESOURCES 14

CHAPTER TWO 19

   BUILDING A SOLID BUSINESS PLAN 19

   IDENTIFYING YOUR BUSINESS GOALS AND OBJECTIVES 19

   DEVELOPING A COMPREHENSIVE BUSINESS PLAN 23

   OUTLINING YOUR MARKETING AND SALES STRATEGIES 26

   CREATING A FINANCIAL PLAN AND BUDGET 29

CHAPTER THREE 33

   ESTABLISHING YOUR BRAND IDENTITY 33

   CREATING A UNIQUE BRAND NAME, LOGO, AND SLOGAN.......................33

   CRAFTING YOUR BRAND MESSAGING AND TONE 36

   DEVELOPING YOUR BRAND STORY AND VALUES 39

   CREATING A CONSISTENT VISUAL IDENTITY...42

   THE IMPORTANCE OF VISUAL CONSISTENCY IN BUILDING A STRONG BRAND IDENTITY 48

CHAPTER FOUR 51

   SETTING UP YOUR BUSINESS INFRASTRUCTURE 51

   CHOOSING A LEGAL STRUCTURE AND REGISTERING YOUR BUSINESS........51

   SETTING UP YOUR WORKSPACE AND EQUIPMENT 56

   UNDERSTANDING TAX REQUIREMENTS AND OBLIGATIONS 59

   HIRING EMPLOYEES AND/OR CONTRACTORS..61

CHAPTER FIVE 65

   LAUNCHING AND GROWING YOUR BUSINESS 65

   LAUNCHING YOUR BUSINESS WITH A BANG 65

   SCALING UP YOUR BUSINESS OVER TIME...70

   DEVELOPING A LOYAL CUSTOMER BASE 72

PROFITS FROM PASSION

MEASURING YOUR BUSINESS SUCCESS AND MAKING ADJUSTMENTS 75

PROFITS FROM PASSION

INTRODUCTION

Have you ever found yourself immersed in a hobby that you just couldn't get enough of? Maybe it's crafting, cooking, photography, or even playing video games. Whatever your hobby may be, it has probably brought you joy, relaxation, and a sense of accomplishment.

But what if I told you that you could turn that hobby into a profitable business? That you could earn money doing something you truly love?

Many successful businesses today started out as simple hobbies. Take Etsy, for example, the online marketplace for handmade goods. It began as a way for founder Rob Kalin to sell his own handmade creations, but quickly grew into a platform for other artisans to sell their unique products as well. Today, Etsy has over 4 million active sellers and generates billions of dollars in annual revenue.

If you have a passion for something and the drive to turn it into a business, you can do it too. But it's not as simple as just selling what you create. There are many factors to consider, from identifying your target audience and competition, to developing a comprehensive business plan, to creating a strong brand and marketing strategy.

This book, "Profits From Passion: Transforming Your Leisure Pursuit into a Profitable Venture," is your guide to making your dream of entrepreneurship a reality. We'll walk you through every step of the process, from evaluating your skills and resources, to choosing a legal structure and registering your business, to launching with a bang.

You'll learn how to identify your target audience and competition, and how to develop a marketing and sales strategy that resonates with your customers. We'll show you how to build a strong brand, with a unique name, logo, and slogan, as well as a compelling brand story and values that will set you apart from the competition.

We'll also cover important topics such as setting up your workspace and equipment, understanding tax requirements and obligations, and hiring employees and/or contractors. And we'll provide tips on how to measure your business success, develop a loyal customer base, and make adjustments along the way to continue growing your business.

Whether you're just starting out or you've been running your hobby as a side hustle for a while and are ready to take it to the next level, this book has everything you need to turn your passion into a profitable business. So let's get started!

PROFITS FROM PASSION

CHAPTER ONE
ASSESSING THE VIABILITY OF YOUR HOBBY AS A BUSINESS

DETERMINING IF THERE IS A MARKET DEMAND FOR YOUR HOBBY

Determining if there is a market demand for your hobby is a critical step when considering turning your hobby into a business. While your passion and love for your hobby are certainly important, it's equally crucial to ensure that there is enough demand for the products or services you plan to offer. In this article, we'll discuss the steps you can take to assess the market demand for your hobby and determine if it's a viable business idea.

1. Conduct Market Research

The first step in assessing market demand is to conduct market research. This involves gathering information about your target audience, competitors, and industry trends. There are several ways to conduct market research, including:

Online research: Use search engines and social media to gather information about your industry, competitors, and target audience. You can also use online surveys and polls to gather feedback from potential customers.

- Offline research: Attend trade shows, conferences, and other industry events to gather information about your industry and network with potential customers and partners.

- Customer interviews: Conduct one-on-one interviews with potential customers to gather feedback about your hobby and understand their needs and preferences.

2. Analyze Industry Trends

Analyzing industry trends is an essential part of market research. This involves looking at the current and future trends in your industry and determining how your hobby fits into those trends. Some of the factors you should consider include:

Market size: Determine the size of the market for your hobby and whether it's growing or shrinking.

- Competition: Analyze the competition in your industry and determine how your hobby compares to your competitors.
- Technology: Determine if any technological advancements could impact your hobby or industry.
- Regulations: Determine if there are any regulations or legal requirements that could impact your hobby or industry.

3. Identify Your Target Audience

Identifying your target audience is another critical step in assessing market demand. Your target audience is the group of people who are most likely to be interested in your hobby and become customers. To identify your target audience, consider the following factors:

Age: Determine the age range of people who are most likely to be interested in your hobby.

- Gender: Determine if your hobby appeals to a specific gender.

- Location: Determine the geographic location of your target audience.
- Income: Determine the income range of your target audience.

4. Determine Customer Needs and Preferences

Once you have identified your target audience, the next step is to determine their needs and preferences. This involves gathering feedback from potential customers and understanding what they are looking for in a product or service. Some of the factors you should consider include:

- Price: Determine how much customers are willing to pay for your products or services.
- Quality: Determine the level of quality that customers expect from your products or services.
- Features: Determine the features that customers are looking for in a product or service.
- Branding: Determine the branding and messaging that resonates with your target audience.

5. Test Your Product or Service

Testing your product or service is a crucial step in determining market demand. This involves creating a prototype or sample of your product or service and testing it with potential customers. Testing your product or service can help you:

- Determine if there is demand for your product or service.
- Identify any issues or areas for improvement.
- Gather feedback from potential customers.

- Determine if your pricing strategy is effective.

UNDERSTANDING YOUR POTENTIAL TARGET AUDIENCE AND COMPETITION

Understanding your potential target audience and competition is essential for any business, regardless of the industry or size. By understanding who your potential customers are and who your competition is, you can make informed decisions about how to market and position your product or service, and how to differentiate yourself from your competitors. In this article, we will explore the importance of understanding your potential target audience and competition, and provide examples and facts to help you gain a better understanding of these concepts.

❖ Understanding Your Potential Target Audience

Your potential target audience is the group of people who are most likely to purchase your product or service. These individuals share common characteristics, such as demographics, interests, needs, and preferences, that make them more likely to be interested in your offering. Understanding your potential target audience is important for several reasons:

It helps you tailor your marketing efforts: By understanding who your potential customers are, you can create targeted marketing campaigns that speak directly to their needs and preferences.

It helps you identify customer needs: Understanding your potential target audience allows you to identify their needs and preferences, which can help you create products or services that meet those needs.

PROFITS FROM PASSION

It helps you improve customer satisfaction: By understanding your potential target audience, you can create products or services that better meet their needs and preferences, which can lead to increased customer satisfaction.

To understand your potential target audience, you should consider the following factors:

- Demographics: Demographics are characteristics such as age, gender, income, education level, and occupation. Understanding the demographics of your potential target audience can help you create products or services that appeal to them.

- Interests: Interests are the things that your potential target audience enjoys, such as hobbies, sports, or entertainment. Understanding their interests can help you create marketing campaigns that speak directly to them.

- Needs and preferences: Understanding the needs and preferences of your potential target audience can help you create products or services that meet their specific needs.

- Behaviors: Understanding the behaviors of your potential target audience can help you create marketing campaigns that appeal to them. For example, if your potential target audience is active on social media, you may want to create social media campaigns to reach them.

Example: Peloton

Peloton is a company that sells high-end exercise equipment and provides virtual fitness classes. Peloton's potential target audience includes individuals who are interested in fitness, have a high disposable income, and enjoy the convenience of working out at home. To appeal to this audience, Peloton creates marketing campaigns that emphasize the convenience of working out at home and the high-quality equipment and virtual classes that it provides. Peloton also creates virtual classes that are tailored to specific interests, such as cycling or yoga, which helps it appeal to a wide range of potential customers.

❖ Understanding Your Competition

Your competition is any other company or individual that provides a similar product or service to yours. Understanding your competition is important for several reasons:

- It helps you differentiate yourself from your competitors: By understanding your competition, you can create a unique selling proposition that sets you apart from your competitors.
- It helps you identify market trends: Understanding your competition can help you identify market trends and adjust your product or service accordingly.
- It helps you stay competitive: Understanding your competition can help you identify areas where you need to improve to stay competitive.

To understand your competition, you should consider the following factors:

- Product or service: What product or service does your competition provide? How is it similar or different from yours?

PROFITS FROM PASSION

- Pricing: How do your competitors price their product or service? Are they more expensive or less expensive than you?
- Marketing: How does your competition market its product or service? What channels do they use to reach their potential customers?
- Unique selling proposition: What is your competition
- Unique selling proposition: What is your competition's unique selling proposition? How do they differentiate themselves from their competitors?
- Strengths and weaknesses: What are your competition's strengths and weaknesses? How can you leverage your strengths to compete more effectively?

Example: Coca-Cola vs. Pepsi

Coca-Cola and Pepsi are two of the most popular soft drink brands in the world. Understanding their competition is crucial for both companies. Both companies offer similar products, but they differentiate themselves in several ways. Coca-Cola is known for its classic taste, iconic branding, and nostalgic appeal. Pepsi, on the other hand, is known for its bold and innovative marketing campaigns, such as its recent partnership with the NFL.

In terms of pricing, both companies are similarly priced. However, Coca-Cola has a larger market share than Pepsi, which means that they have a stronger brand presence in the soft drink market. Coca-Cola has also diversified its product line, offering a variety of different soft drinks and beverages to appeal to different audiences.

In terms of marketing, both companies use a variety of channels to reach their potential customers, including television, print, and social media. Coca-Cola's marketing campaigns often focus on nostalgia and the emotional connection that people have with the brand, while Pepsi's campaigns are often more focused on pop culture and current events.

In conclusion, understanding your potential target audience and competition is critical for the success of any business. By understanding who your potential customers are and who your competitors are, you can create targeted marketing campaigns, identify customer needs, and differentiate yourself from your competitors. Examples such as Peloton and Coca-Cola demonstrate the importance of understanding your potential target audience and competition to succeed in a competitive market.

EVALUATING YOUR SKILLS AND RESOURCES

Evaluating your skills and resources is an important step in determining whether your hobby can become a viable business. It involves taking a critical look at your strengths and weaknesses, as well as the resources that are available to you, to determine whether you have what it takes to turn your hobby into a successful business venture.

Skills Assessment

PROFITS FROM PASSION

The first step in evaluating your skills is to identify the skills that are necessary to run a successful business. These skills will vary depending on the type of business you are starting, but some general skills that are important for any entrepreneur to possess include:

- ✓ Communication Skills: As an entrepreneur, you will need to communicate effectively with customers, employees, suppliers, and other stakeholders. This involves being able to clearly articulate your vision and goals, as well as being able to listen and respond to feedback.
- ✓ Leadership Skills: Starting a business requires strong leadership skills, as you will need to make tough decisions, motivate employees, and manage day-to-day operations.
- ✓ Financial Skills: As a business owner, you will need to have a basic understanding of accounting and finance to manage cash flow, create budgets, and make informed financial decisions.
- ✓ Marketing Skills: To attract customers and grow your business, you will need to have a basic understanding of marketing and sales.
- ✓ Time Management Skills: Starting a business can be time-consuming, so it is important to be able to manage your time effectively to balance your business and personal life.

Once you have identified the skills that are necessary for running a successful business, you should take an honest assessment of your skills and experience. Identify areas where you are strong and areas where you may need to improve. This will help you determine whether you have the necessary skills to turn your hobby into a successful business.

Resource Assessment

In addition to evaluating your skills, you should also evaluate the resources that are available to you. Resources can include:

- ✓ Financial Resources: Starting a business often requires an initial investment of money. Do you have the financial resources necessary to get your business off the ground?
- ✓ Human Resources: Running a successful business often requires a team of dedicated employees. Do you have the necessary skills to manage and motivate employees? Do you have a network of contacts who can help you find qualified employees?
- ✓ Physical Resources: Depending on the type of business you are starting, you may need access to physical resources such as office space, equipment, and inventory. Do you have access to the physical resources necessary to start your business?
- ✓ Intellectual Resources: Running a successful business often requires access to knowledge and expertise. Do you have access to industry experts who can provide guidance and support? Are there industry associations or trade organizations that you can join to gain access to resources and support?
- ✓ Time Resources: Starting a business can be time-consuming. Do you have the necessary time to dedicate to starting and growing your business?

PROFITS FROM PASSION

Examples of Evaluating Skills and Resources

1. Amazon

Jeff Bezos, the founder of Amazon, recognized that his skills in computer science and business management could be leveraged to create a successful online retail business. He also recognized the potential of the internet as a tool for reaching a global audience. With these skills and resources in mind, he launched Amazon in 1994 as an online bookstore. Today, Amazon is one of the largest online retailers in the world, offering a wide range of products and services.

2. Airbnb

Airbnb was founded by Brian Chesky and Joe Gebbia, who recognized a need for affordable short-term rentals in San Francisco. They leveraged their design and marketing skills to create a website that allowed people to rent out their homes to travelers. With their initial success in San Francisco, they expanded their business globally. Today, Airbnb is a multi-the billion-dollar company that operates in more than 220 countries and has over 150 million users.

3. Patagonia

Patagonia is a clothing company that was founded by Yvon Chouinard in 1973. Chouinard was an avid outdoorsman who recognized a need for high-quality outdoor clothing. He leveraged his own experience and skills in rock climbing and mountaineering to create a line of durable and functional outdoor clothing. Today, Patagonia is known for its commitment to sustainability and ethical business practices.

4. Sweetgreen

Sweetgreen is a fast-casual restaurant chain that was founded by three friends who recognized a need for healthy, convenient food options. They leveraged their skills in business and marketing to create a brand that resonated with health-conscious consumers. Today, Sweetgreen has more than 100 locations across the United States and has been valued at over $1 billion.

5. Warby Parker

Warby Parker was founded by four friends who recognized a need for affordable, stylish eyewear. They leveraged their skills in design, marketing, and e-commerce to create a business model that disrupted the traditional eyewear industry. Today, Warby Parker is valued at over $1 billion and has become a popular brand among millennials and other young consumers. Evaluating your skills and resources is an important step in determining whether your hobby can become a successful business. By taking a critical look at your strengths and weaknesses, as well as the resources that are available to you, you can determine whether you have what it takes to turn your hobby into a viable business venture. Examples of successful businesses such as Amazon, Airbnb, Patagonia, Sweetgreen, and Warby Parker demonstrate how leveraging your skills and resources can lead to successful entrepreneurship.

CHAPTER TWO
BUILDING A SOLID BUSINESS PLAN
IDENTIFYING YOUR BUSINESS GOALS AND OBJECTIVES

Starting a business requires more than just a good idea. It requires a solid understanding of your business goals and objectives. Setting clear goals and objectives is essential for creating a roadmap to success and staying focused on what you want to achieve. In this article, we will explore how to identify your business goals and objectives and provide examples of successful companies that have done so.

WHAT ARE BUSINESS GOALS AND OBJECTIVES?

Business goals are specific targets that a company sets to achieve within a given timeframe. They are typically long-term and broad in scope, providing direction for the company's overall strategy. Business objectives, on the other hand, are specific, measurable, and time-bound steps that a company takes to achieve its goals. Objectives are the actionable steps that a company takes to reach its goals.

Identifying Your Business Goals

To identify your business goals, you need to start by thinking about what you want to achieve with your business. This can involve asking yourself some tough questions, such as:

- What is the purpose of your business?
- What are your long-term aspirations?
- What do you want to be known for in your industry?
- How will you measure success?

PROFITS FROM PASSION

Once you have a clear idea of what you want to achieve, you can begin to set your business goals. Business goals should be specific, measurable, achievable, relevant, and time-bound (SMART). Here are some examples of business goals:

o Increase Revenue

One of the most common business goals is to increase revenue. This can be achieved in many ways, such as by increasing sales, expanding into new markets, or launching new products or services. For example, Amazon's goal is to become the world's most customer-centric company by offering a wide range of products, low prices, and fast delivery.

o Build Brand Awareness

Building brand awareness is another common business goal. This involves creating a strong brand identity and communicating it effectively to your target audience. For example, Nike's goal is to inspire and innovate every athlete in the world by creating high-quality products and engaging with customers through social media and other marketing channels.

o Improve Customer Satisfaction

Improving customer satisfaction is a business goal that can help you retain customers and increase revenue. This involves delivering high-quality products and services and providing excellent customer service. For example, Zappos' goal is to provide the best online shopping experience by offering free shipping, easy returns, and 24/7 customer support.

Identifying Your Business Objectives

Once you have identified your business goals, you need to set objectives to help you achieve them. Business objectives should be specific, measurable, achievable, relevant, and time-bound (SMART). Here are some examples of business objectives:

Increase Sales by 10% in the Next Quarter

To achieve the goal of increasing revenue, you could set the objective of increasing sales by 10% in the next quarter. This could involve launching a new marketing campaign, expanding into new markets, or improving your sales process.

Increase Social Media Engagement by 20% in the Next Month

To achieve the goal of building brand awareness, you could set the objective of increasing social media engagement by 20% in the next month. This could involve creating more engaging social media content, running a social media contest, or partnering with influencers to promote your brand.

Improve Customer Service Response Time to Under 24 Hours

To achieve the goal of improving customer satisfaction, you could set the objective of improving your customer service response time to under 24 hours. This could involve hiring more customer service representatives, implementing a customer service chatbot, or improving your customer service processes.

Determine Your Unique Selling Proposition

Your unique selling proposition (USP) is what sets your product or service apart from your competitors. Determining your USP is essential in assessing market demand because it helps you understand why customers would choose your product or service over your competitors. To determine your USP, consider the following factors:

- What makes your product or service unique?
- What value do you offer that your competitors don't?
- What problems does your product or service solve for customers?
- What benefits do customers receive from using your product or service?

By answering these questions, you can determine your USP and use it to differentiate your product or service in the market.

Estimate Your Sales Potential

Finally, once you have gathered all the necessary information, you can estimate your sales potential. This involves projecting the number of customers you can expect to attract and the revenue you can generate. To estimate your sales potential, consider the following factors:

- Market size: Determine the size of the market for your hobby and estimate the percentage of customers you can attract.
- Competition: Analyze the competition in your industry and determine how much market share you can capture.
- Customer needs: Determine the needs and preferences of your target audience and estimate how many customers are likely to purchase your product or service.

- Pricing: Determine your pricing strategy and estimate how much revenue you can generate based on your projected sales volume.

By estimating your sales potential, you can determine if there is enough demand for your hobby to turn it into a profitable business.

In conclusion, determining market demand is a critical step in turning your hobby into a business. By conducting market research, analyzing industry trends, identifying your target audience, determining customer needs and preferences, testing your product or service, determining your unique selling proposition, and estimating your sales potential, you can assess the viability of your hobby as a business idea. With this information, you can make an informed decision about whether or not to pursue your hobby as a business and set yourself up for success.

DEVELOPING A COMPREHENSIVE BUSINESS PLAN

Developing a comprehensive business plan is crucial to the success of any business. It provides a roadmap for how you plan to run and grow your business, identifies potential challenges and risks, and outlines strategies for overcoming them. In this article, we will explore the key components of a comprehensive business plan and provide examples of successful companies that have developed effective business plans.

1. Executive Summary

The executive summary is the first section of your business plan, and it provides an overview of your business. It should include a brief description of your company, the products or services you offer, your target market, and your goals and objectives. The executive summary should also highlight the key points of your business plan.

2. Company Description

The company description provides a more detailed overview of your company. It should include information about your company's history, ownership structure, and legal status. You should also provide information about your products or services, your target market, and your competitive advantage.

3. Market Analysis

The market analysis section of your business plan should provide a detailed analysis of your target market. This includes information about the size of your target market, the demographics of your target audience, and any trends or challenges in the market. You should also identify your competitors and analyze their strengths and weaknesses.

4. Marketing and Sales Strategies

The marketing and sales strategies section of your business plan should outline how you plan to market and sell your products or services. This includes information about your pricing strategy, your distribution channels, and your promotional activities. You should also identify your sales team and provide information about their experience and qualifications.

5. Product or Service Line

The product or service line section of your business plan should provide detailed information about the products or services you offer. This includes information about the features and benefits of your products or services, as well as any patents or trademarks you hold. You should also provide information about your production process, including any suppliers or vendors you work with.

6. Management Team

The management team section of your business plan should provide information about the key members of your management team. This includes information about their experience, qualifications, and responsibilities. You should also provide information about any advisors or consultants you work with.

7. Financial Projections

The financial projections section of your business plan should provide detailed information about your financial projections. This includes information about your revenue and expenses, as well as any funding or financing you plan to secure. You should also include a cash flow statement, balance sheet, and income statement.

Conclusion

Developing a comprehensive business plan is essential to the success of any business. It provides a roadmap for how you plan to run and grow your business, identifies potential challenges and risks, and outlines strategies for overcoming them. By including key components such as an executive summary, company description, market analysis, marketing and sales strategies, product or service line, management team, and financial projections, you can create a comprehensive business plan that sets your business up for success.

OUTLINING YOUR MARKETING AND SALES STRATEGIES

Marketing and sales strategies are critical components of any successful business plan. They help you identify your target market, create brand awareness, and increase sales. In this article, we will discuss the key components of an effective marketing and sales strategy and provide examples of companies that have developed successful strategies.

A. Target Market

The first step in developing a marketing and sales strategy is identifying your target market. This includes understanding their needs, interests, and purchasing behaviors. You can gather this information through market research, surveys, and customer feedback.

Example: Nike

Nike's target market is athletes and sports enthusiasts. They have a deep understanding of their customer's needs and interests, and they tailor their marketing and sales strategies to appeal to them.

B. Brand Positioning

Once you have identified your target market, the next step is to position your brand in a way that resonates with them. This includes identifying your unique selling proposition (USP) and creating a brand personality that aligns with your target market's values and beliefs.

Example: Apple

PROFITS FROM PASSION

Apple's USP is its innovative and user-friendly technology. They have created a brand personality that is sleek, modern, and cutting-edge, which resonates with their target market of tech-savvy individuals.

   C. Marketing Mix

The marketing mix is a set of tactics that businesses use to promote their products or services. It includes the four Ps: product, price, promotion, and place. A successful marketing mix requires a balance between these elements.

- Product: This includes the features, benefits, and quality of your product or service.
- Price: This includes your pricing strategy, such as premium pricing or value pricing.
- Promotion: This includes your promotional activities, such as advertising, public relations, and sales promotions.
- Place: This includes your distribution channels, such as direct sales, retail sales, or online sales.

Example: Coca-Cola

Coca-Cola's marketing mix includes high-quality products, premium pricing, and extensive advertising campaigns. They also have a strong distribution network, which allows them to reach consumers all over the world.

   D. Sales Strategies

Sales strategies are the tactics businesses use to sell their products or services. This includes identifying potential customers, creating sales pitches, and building relationships with customers.

PROFITS FROM PASSION

Example: Amazon

Amazon's sales strategy includes a user-friendly website, personalized recommendations, and fast shipping. They also have a loyalty program, Amazon Prime, which offers exclusive discounts and perks to members.

E. Digital Marketing

In today's digital age, digital marketing is an essential component of any marketing and sales strategy. This includes social media marketing, email marketing, search engine optimization (SEO), and content marketing.

Example: Airbnb

Airbnb's digital marketing strategy includes a user-friendly website, extensive social media presence, and personalized email campaigns. They also use content marketing, such as blog posts and city guides, to provide value to their customers and build brand awareness.

Conclusion

Marketing and sales strategies are essential components of any successful business. By identifying your target market, positioning your brand, creating a balanced marketing mix, developing effective sales strategies, and incorporating digital marketing tactics, you can increase brand awareness and drive sales. By learning from successful companies such as Nike, Apple, Coca-Cola, Amazon, and Airbnb, you can develop a marketing and sales strategy that sets your business up for success.

CREATING A FINANCIAL PLAN AND BUDGET

Creating a financial plan and budget is an important aspect of running a successful business. A financial plan outlines the financial goals and objectives of the business, while a budget lays out a plan for allocating resources to achieve those goals. In this article, we will discuss the key components of a comprehensive financial plan and budget, and provide examples of successful companies that have developed effective financial plans and budgets.

Assessing Your Financial Situation

Before you can develop a financial plan and budget, you need to assess your current financial situation. This includes analyzing your income, expenses, cash flow, and debt. You can use financial statements, such as income statements, balance sheets, and cash flow statements, to get a clear picture of your financial situation.

Example: Apple

Apple's financial statements show strong financial performance, with consistent revenue growth and healthy profit margins. They also have a large cash reserve, which they use for research and development, acquisitions, and share buybacks.

Setting Financial Goals and Objectives

Once you have assessed your financial situation, you can set financial goals and objectives for your business. This includes identifying specific financial targets, such as revenue, profit, and cash flow, and setting a timeline for achieving them.

Example: Amazon

PROFITS FROM PASSION

Amazon's financial goals include revenue growth, profitability, and cash flow. They have set aggressive growth targets, such as expanding their Prime membership program and entering new markets, and they have consistently met or exceeded their financial targets.

⬇ Creating a Budget

A budget is a plan for allocating resources to achieve your financial goals and objectives. It includes projected revenue, expenses, and cash flow, as well as a breakdown of how resources will be allocated among different areas of the business.

Example: McDonald's

McDonald's has a comprehensive budget that includes projections for revenue, expenses, and cash flow. They also have a detailed breakdown of how resources will be allocated among different areas of the business, such as marketing, research and development, and capital expenditures.

⬇ Managing Cash Flow

Cash flow is the lifeblood of any business, and managing cash flow effectively is crucial for long-term success. This includes forecasting cash flow, monitoring actual cash flow, and taking action to improve cash flow when necessary.

Example: Microsoft

Microsoft has a strong cash flow management strategy, which includes forecasting cash flow, monitoring actual cash flow, and taking action to improve cash flow when necessary. They have also implemented measures to reduce working capital, such as optimizing inventory levels and improving accounts receivable management.

+ Managing Debt

Debt can be a useful tool for financing growth and expansion, but it can also be a liability if not managed properly. This includes understanding the types of debt available, such as loans, lines of credit, and bonds, and developing a strategy for managing debt.

Example: Tesla

Tesla has used debt strategically to finance their growth and expansion, such as building new factories and developing new products. They have also implemented measures to manage debt, such as refinancing debt at lower interest rates and reducing debt levels through equity offerings.

+ Investing in the Future

Investing in the future is essential for long-term success. This includes investing in research and development, capital expenditures, and acquisitions, as well as developing a strategy for managing investments.

Example: Alphabet (Google)

Alphabet (Google) has a comprehensive investment strategy, which includes investing in research and development, capital expenditures, and acquisitions. They also have a detailed strategy for managing investments, such as balancing investments in core businesses with investments in emerging technologies.

Conclusion

PROFITS FROM PASSION

Creating a financial plan and budget is a critical component of running a successful business. By assessing your financial situation, setting financial goals and objectives, creating a budget, managing cash flow and debt, and investing in the future, you can achieve long-term financial success. By learning from successful companies such as Apple, Amazon , McDonald's, Microsoft, Tesla, and Alphabet (Google), you can gain insights into effective financial planning and budgeting strategies. Remember to regularly review and adjust your financial plan and budget as needed to ensure that you are on track to achieve your financial goals and objectives.

CHAPTER THREE
ESTABLISHING YOUR BRAND IDENTITY
CREATING A UNIQUE BRAND NAME, LOGO, AND SLOGAN

Creating a unique brand name, logo, and slogan is an important part of establishing a strong brand identity for your business. A strong brand identity helps distinguish your business from competitors, builds customer loyalty, and creates a memorable impression. In this article, we will discuss the key components of creating a unique brand name, logo, and slogan, and provide examples of successful companies that have developed strong brand identities.

➢ Choosing a Unique Brand Name

A brand name is the primary identifier for your business and should reflect the essence of your brand. A unique brand name is important because it helps your business stand out in a crowded market, and makes it easier for customers to remember and recognize your brand.

Example: Google

Google's brand name is a unique and memorable play on the word "googol," which represents the number 1 followed by 100 zeros. The name reflects the company's focus on organizing and making sense of vast amounts of data on the internet.

➢ Designing a Memorable Logo

A logo is a graphical representation of your brand and should be designed to reflect your brand's identity and values. A memorable logo is important because it helps customers recognize and remember your brand, and can serve as a visual representation of your brand in marketing materials.

Example: Nike

Nike's "swoosh" logo is a simple, memorable design that has become synonymous with the brand. The design represents the brand's focus on movement and athleticism and has helped Nike establish a strong brand identity.

> ➢ Developing a Memorable Slogan

A slogan is a memorable phrase that captures the essence of your brand and communicates it to customers. A memorable slogan is important because it helps customers remember your brand and associate it with key attributes and values.

Example: McDonald's

McDonald's "I'm Lovin' It" slogan is a memorable and catchy phrase that has become synonymous with the brand. The slogan communicates the brand's focus on providing enjoyable dining experiences and has helped establish McDonald's as a leader in the fast-food industry.

> ➢ Creating a Consistent Brand Identity

Once you have developed a unique brand name, logo, and slogan, it is important to maintain consistency across all brand touchpoints. This includes using consistent visual and verbal language in marketing materials, advertising, and customer communications.

Example: Coca-Cola

Coca-Cola has developed a consistent brand identity across all touchpoints, using consistent visual and verbal language in marketing materials, advertising, and customer communications. The brand's signature red and white color scheme, along with its "Taste the Feeling" slogan, has become synonymous with the brand and has helped establish Coca-Cola as a leader in the beverage industry.

➤ Building Brand Awareness

Building brand awareness is essential for establishing a strong brand identity and driving business growth. This includes developing a marketing strategy that reaches your target audience through a variety of channels, such as social media, advertising, and content marketing.

Example: Apple

Apple has developed a comprehensive marketing strategy that reaches its target audience through a variety of channels, such as social media, advertising, and content marketing. The brand's focus on sleek, modern design and innovative technology has helped establish Apple as a leader in the tech industry.

➤ Creating a Unique Brand Experience

Creating a unique brand experience is essential for establishing customer loyalty and driving business growth. This includes developing a brand voice and tone that reflects your brand's personality and values, as well as providing exceptional customer service and experiences.

Example: Starbucks

Starbucks has created a unique brand experience that reflects its commitment to providing exceptional coffee and customer service. The brand's friendly and welcoming atmosphere, along with its commitment to ethical and sustainable sourcing, has helped establish Starbucks as a leader in the coffee industry.

CRAFTING YOUR BRAND MESSAGING AND TONE

Crafting your brand messaging and tone is an essential step in establishing a strong brand identity for your business. Your brand messaging communicates your brand's values, personality, and unique selling proposition to your target audience, while your tone sets the emotional tone of your brand communications. In this article, we will discuss the key components of crafting your brand messaging and tone, including identifying your brand values, defining your unique selling proposition, and developing a brand voice and tone. We will also provide examples of successful brands that have developed strong brand messaging and tone.

➤ Identifying Your Brand Values

Your brand values are the principles and beliefs that guide your business and shape your brand identity. Identifying your brand values is important because it helps you communicate your brand's personality and unique selling proposition to your target audience. Your brand values should be aligned with the needs and values of your target audience and should be reflected in all aspects of your brand communications.

Example: Patagonia

Patagonia is a clothing brand that has developed a strong brand identity around its commitment to sustainability and environmentalism. The brand's values are reflected in its product design, sourcing, and marketing communications, which emphasize the brand's commitment to minimizing its environmental impact.

> ➢ Defining Your Unique Selling Proposition

Your unique selling proposition (USP) is the unique benefit that your brand provides to your target audience. Defining your USP is important because it helps you differentiate your brand from competitors and communicate your brand's value to your target audience. Your USP should be aligned with your brand values and should be communicated in all aspects of your brand messaging.

Example: Dollar Shave Club

Dollar Shave Club is a shaving subscription service that has developed a strong USP around its affordable and convenient service. The brand's messaging emphasizes its unique value proposition of providing high-quality razors and grooming products at an affordable price, which has helped the brand differentiate itself from competitors in the crowded shaving market.

> ➢ Developing a Brand Voice and Tone

Your brand voice and tone are the emotional and linguistic characteristics that define your brand's personality and communication style. Developing a consistent brand voice and tone is important because it helps you build brand awareness and recognition, and establish an emotional connection with your target audience.

Example: Airbnb

PROFITS FROM PASSION

Airbnb has developed a distinctive brand voice and tone that reflects the brand's values of community, diversity, and inclusion. The brand's messaging is characterized by a friendly and inclusive tone, which is reflected in its advertising, social media, and customer communications.

➤ Crafting a Brand Messaging Framework

Crafting a brand messaging framework is an essential step in developing a comprehensive brand messaging strategy. A brand messaging framework includes the key messages and brand story that define your brand identity, as well as the tone and language that should be used in all brand communications.

Example: Nike

Nike has developed a comprehensive brand messaging framework that includes it is iconic "Just Do It" slogan and brand story of inspiring athletes to achieve their goals. The brand's messaging framework is reflected in all aspects of its marketing communications, from advertising to social media to customer service.

➤ Testing and Refining Your Brand Messaging

Testing and refining your brand messaging is an ongoing process that helps you ensure that your messaging is resonating with your target audience and driving business growth. This includes conducting market research, analyzing customer feedback, and tracking key performance indicators to evaluate the effectiveness of your brand messaging strategy.

Example: Coca-Cola

PROFITS FROM PASSION

Coca-Cola has a long history of testing and refining its brand messaging strategy, from its iconic "Share a Coke" campaign to its recent "Taste the Feeling" campaign. The brand's ongoing commitment to testing and refining its messaging strategy has helped it maintain its position as a leader in the beverage industry.

DEVELOPING YOUR BRAND STORY AND VALUES

Developing your brand story and values is an important aspect of building a strong brand identity. Your brand story is the narrative that tells the story of your brand's history, values, and mission, while your brand values are the guiding principles that inform your business decisions and shape your brand identity. In this article, we will discuss the key components of developing your brand story and values, including identifying your brand purpose, defining your brand personality, and developing a brand narrative. We will also provide examples of successful brands that have developed strong brand stories and values.

➢ Identifying Your Brand Purpose

Your brand purpose is the reason why your business exists beyond making a profit. It is the underlying mission that drives your business decisions and shapes your brand identity. Identifying your brand purpose is important because it helps you communicate your brand's values and mission to your target audience, and establishes an emotional connection with your customers.

Example: TOMS Shoes

PROFITS FROM PASSION

TOMS Shoes is a footwear brand that has developed a strong brand purpose around its commitment to giving back. For every pair of shoes purchased, the company donates a pair of shoes to a child in need. The brand's purpose is reflected in its messaging and marketing communications, which emphasize the brand's commitment to making a positive impact in the world.

> ➢ Defining Your Brand Personality

Your brand personality is the set of human characteristics that define your brand's identity and shape how your target audience perceives your brand. Defining your brand personality is important because it helps you create a emotional connection with your target audience, and differentiate your brand from competitors.

Example: Apple

Apple is a technology brand that has developed a strong brand personality around its innovative and creative spirit. The brand's messaging and marketing communications emphasize the brand's commitment to pushing the boundaries of what is possible in technology and creating products that are both functional and beautiful.

> ➢ Developing a Brand Narrative

Your brand narrative is the story that tells the history, values, and mission of your brand. Developing a brand narrative is important because it helps you communicate your brand's story to your target audience, and establish an emotional connection with your customers.

Example: Patagonia

PROFITS FROM PASSION

Patagonia is a clothing brand that has developed a strong brand narrative around its commitment to sustainability and environmentalism. The brand's messaging and marketing communications emphasize the brand's history of supporting environmental causes and its commitment to minimizing its environmental impact through sustainable product design and sourcing.

➤ Communicating Your Brand Story and Values
Communicating your brand story and values is an ongoing process that involves developing a comprehensive brand messaging strategy that communicates your brand's values and mission to your target audience. This includes developing a messaging framework, creating marketing communications that align with your brand's personality and values, and engaging with your customers to build an emotional connection with your brand.

Example: Coca-Cola
Coca-Cola is a beverage brand that has developed a comprehensive brand messaging strategy that communicates its brand story and values to its target audience. The brand's messaging framework emphasizes its history of creating shared experiences and promoting happiness, while its marketing communications focus on creating emotional connections with its customers through storytelling and engaging content.

➤ Measuring the Impact of Your Brand Story and Values
Measuring the impact of your brand story and values is an important aspect of developing a comprehensive brand

messaging strategy. This includes tracking key performance indicators, such as brand awareness, customer engagement, and revenue growth, to evaluate the effectiveness of your brand messaging and make data-driven decisions to improve your brand identity.

Example: Airbnb

Airbnb has developed a data-driven approach to measuring the impact of its brand story and values. The brand uses a range of metrics, including customer feedback and social media engagement, to evaluate the effectiveness of its messaging strategy and make data-driven decisions to improve its brand identity.

CREATING A CONSISTENT VISUAL IDENTITY

Developing your brand story and values is an important aspect of building a strong brand identity. Your brand story is the narrative that tells the story of your brand's history, values, and mission, while your brand values are the guiding principles that inform your business decisions and shape your brand identity. In this article, we will discuss the key components of developing your brand story and values, including identifying your brand purpose, defining your brand personality, and developing a brand narrative. We will also provide examples of successful brands that have developed strong brand stories and values.

➢ Identifying Your Brand Purpose

Your brand purpose is the reason why your business exists beyond making a profit. It is the underlying mission that drives your business decisions and shapes your brand identity.

PROFITS FROM PASSION

Identifying your brand purpose is important because it helps you communicate your brand's values and mission to your target audience, and establishes an emotional connection with your customers.

Example: TOMS Shoes

TOMS Shoes is a footwear brand that has developed a strong brand purpose around its commitment to giving back. For every pair of shoes purchased, the company donates a pair of shoes to a child in need. The brand's purpose is reflected in its messaging and marketing communications, which emphasize the brand's commitment to making a positive impact in the world.

➢ Defining Your Brand Personality

Your brand personality is the set of human characteristics that define your brand's identity and shape how your target audience perceives your brand. Defining your brand personality is important because it helps you create a emotional connection with your target audience, and differentiate your brand from competitors.

Example: Apple

Apple is a technology brand that has developed a strong brand personality around its innovative and creative spirit. The brand's messaging and marketing communications emphasize the brand's commitment to pushing the boundaries of what is possible in technology and creating products that are both functional and beautiful.

➢ Developing a Brand Narrative

PROFITS FROM PASSION

Your brand narrative is the story that tells the history, values, and mission of your brand. Developing a brand narrative is important because it helps you communicate your brand's story to your target audience, and establish an emotional connection with your customers.

Example: Patagonia

Patagonia is a clothing brand that has developed a strong brand narrative around its commitment to sustainability and environmentalism. The brand's messaging and marketing communications emphasize the brand's history of supporting environmental causes and its commitment to minimizing its environmental impact through sustainable product design and sourcing.

➢ Communicating Your Brand Story and Values

Communicating your brand story and values is an ongoing process that involves developing a comprehensive brand messaging strategy that communicates your brand's values and mission to your target audience. This includes developing a messaging framework, creating marketing communications that align with your brand's personality and values, and engaging with your customers to build an emotional connection with your brand.

Example: Coca-Cola

Coca-Cola is a beverage brand that has developed a comprehensive brand messaging strategy that communicates its brand story and values to its target audience. The brand's messaging framework emphasizes its history of creating shared experiences and promoting happiness, while its marketing communications focus on creating emotional connections with its customers through storytelling and engaging content.

➢ Measuring the Impact of Your Brand Story and Values
Measuring the impact of your brand story and values is an important aspect of developing a comprehensive brand messaging strategy. This includes tracking key performance indicators, such as brand awareness, customer engagement, and revenue growth, to evaluate the effectiveness of your brand messaging and make data-driven decisions to improve your brand identity.

Example: Airbnb
Airbnb has developed a data-driven approach to measuring the impact of its brand story and values. The brand uses a range of metrics, including customer feedback and social media engagement, to evaluate the effectiveness of its messaging strategy and make data-driven decisions to improve its brand identity.

Creating a consistent visual identity is an important aspect of building a strong brand image. Your visual identity is the collection of visual elements that represent your brand, including your logo, color scheme, typography, and graphic elements. Developing a consistent visual identity is important because it helps your target audience recognize your brand across different channels and touchpoints, and establishes a sense of brand familiarity and trust. In this article, we will discuss the key components of creating a consistent visual identity, including developing a brand style guide, selecting a color palette, and designing a logo. We will also provide insights from researchers and design experts on the importance of visual consistency in building a strong brand identity.

➢ Developing a Brand Style Guide

A brand style guide is a document that outlines the visual and design elements that define your brand identity. It includes guidelines for your logo, typography, color palette, and other graphic elements, as well as instructions on how to use these elements consistently across different channels and touchpoints. Developing a brand style guide is important because it ensures that your visual identity is consistent and cohesive, and helps your target audience recognize your brand more easily.

Example: Starbucks

Starbucks is a coffee chain that has developed a strong brand style guide that defines its visual identity across different touchpoints. The brand's style guide includes guidelines for its logo, typography, color palette, and graphic elements, as well as instructions on how to use these elements consistently across its stores, packaging, and marketing communications.

➢ Selecting a Color Palette

Selecting a color palette is an important aspect of developing a consistent visual identity. Your color palette is the collection of colors that represent your brand, and it plays a key role in shaping your brand personality and evoking emotions in your target audience. Selecting a color palette that is consistent with your brand values and personality is important because it helps your target audience recognize your brand more easily, and establishes an emotional connection with your customers.

Example: Coca-Cola

Coca-Cola is a beverage brand that has developed a strong color palette that is consistent with its brand values and personality. The brand's color palette includes the signature red and white colors, which evoke emotions of happiness, joy, and excitement. The brand uses these colors consistently across its packaging, marketing communications, and stores, creating a strong sense of brand recognition and familiarity.

➤ Designing a Logo

Designing a logo is another important aspect of creating a consistent visual identity. Your logo is the primary visual element that represents your brand, and it plays a key role in shaping your brand identity and establishing an emotional connection with your target audience. Designing a logo that is simple, memorable, and consistent with your brand values and personality is important because it helps your target audience recognize your brand more easily, and establishes a sense of brand familiarity and trust.

Example: Nike

Nike is a sportswear brand that has developed a strong logo that is consistent with its brand values and personality. The brand's logo is simple, memorable, and recognizable, featuring the iconic "swoosh" graphic and the brand name in bold typography. The brand uses this logo consistently across its packaging, marketing communications, and products, creating a strong sense of brand recognition and familiarity.

THE IMPORTANCE OF VISUAL CONSISTENCY IN BUILDING A STRONG BRAND IDENTITY

Visual consistency is a key factor in building a strong brand identity. Consistent use of visual elements and design principles helps to create a sense of familiarity and trust in your target audience and establishes an emotional connection with your customers. Researchers and design experts have highlighted the importance of visual consistency in building a strong brand identity.

Research has shown that visual consistency is a key factor in building brand recognition and familiarity. According to a study by the Nielsen Norman Group, visual consistency across different touchpoints can increase brand recognition by up to 80%. This means that developing

Visual identity includes elements such as logo design, color palette, typography, imagery, and other design elements that create a recognizable and cohesive look and feel for a brand. Developing a consistent visual identity requires careful consideration and planning to ensure that all elements work together to effectively communicate the brand's message and values.

To develop a consistent visual identity, it's important to start with a clear understanding of the brand's personality, target audience, and values. This will inform the design choices and ensure that they align with the brand's overall message and goals.

One of the first steps in developing a consistent visual identity is to create a brand style guide. This document outlines the visual elements of the brand, including the logo, color palette, typography, and any other design elements. It also provides guidelines for how these elements should be used across different touchpoints, such as websites, social media profiles, marketing materials, and packaging.

The logo is often the most recognizable visual element of a brand and is a key component of the visual identity. A well-designed logo should be simple, memorable, and communicate the brand's message and personality. It should also be versatile enough to be used across different mediums and sizes.

The color palette is another important aspect of a brand's visual identity. Colors can evoke emotions and associations, and choosing the right colors can help communicate the brand's message and personality. For example, blue is often associated with trust and reliability, while red can evoke excitement and passion. A consistent color palette should be used across all touchpoints to create a cohesive and recognizable look and feel.

Typography is another important design element that can contribute to the brand's visual identity. The choice of font can communicate the brand's personality and tone, whether it's playful and fun or serious and professional. It's important to choose a font that is easy to read and works well across different mediums.

PROFITS FROM PASSION

Imagery is also a key component of a brand's visual identity. Whether it's product photography, lifestyle images, or graphics, the imagery should be consistent with the brand's message and values. It's important to choose imagery that resonates with the target audience and communicates the brand's personality.

In addition to these design elements, it's important to consider how the visual identity will be implemented across different touchpoints. This includes websites, social media profiles, marketing materials, and packaging. Consistency across these touchpoints is essential for building brand recognition and familiarity.

Overall, developing a consistent visual identity requires careful consideration and planning to ensure that all elements work together to effectively communicate the brand's message and values. By creating a brand style guide and considering all design elements, a strong and recognizable visual identity can be developed, helping to build a strong and memorable brand.

CHAPTER FOUR
SETTING UP YOUR BUSINESS INFRASTRUCTURE
CHOOSING A LEGAL STRUCTURE AND REGISTERING YOUR BUSINESS

When starting a business, one of the key decisions you'll need to make is choosing a legal structure and registering your business. This decision will have important legal and financial implications, so it's important to do your research and choose the structure that best suits your business's needs.

There are several legal structures to choose from, each with its advantages and disadvantages. The most common structures are sole proprietorship, partnership, limited liability company (LLC), and corporation.

The sole proprietorship is the simplest legal structure and is suitable for small businesses with a single owner. With this structure, the business owner is personally responsible for all aspects of the business, including debts and legal liabilities. This structure offers the most flexibility and the least amount of paperwork but also carries the most risk.

The partnership is similar to a sole proprietorship but involves multiple owners. In this structure, all partners share in the profits and losses of the business, and each partner is personally liable for the debts and legal liabilities of the business. It's important to have a solid partnership agreement in place to outline each partner's responsibilities and protect the business in case of disagreements.

PROFITS FROM PASSION

LLC is a popular structure for small businesses as it provides the liability protection of a corporation while maintaining the flexibility and tax benefits of a partnership. With an LLC, the business is a separate legal entity, meaning that the owners are not personally liable for the business's debts or legal liabilities. However, setting up an LLC involves more paperwork and fees than a sole proprietorship or partnership.

The corporation is a more complex legal structure that offers the most liability protection for the owners. With a corporation, the business is a separate legal entity and the owners are not personally liable for the business's debts or legal liabilities. However, this structure involves more paperwork and fees than the other structures and requires annual meetings and other formalities.

When choosing a legal structure for your business, it's important to consider factors such as liability protection, tax implications, and paperwork requirements. It's also important to consult with a lawyer or accountant to ensure that you choose the structure that best suits your business's needs.

Once you've chosen a legal structure, you'll need to register your business with the appropriate government agencies. This typically involves registering with the state government and obtaining any necessary licenses and permits. Depending on your industry and location, you may also need to register with federal agencies such as the Internal Revenue Service (IRS) or the Securities and Exchange Commission (SEC).

PROFITS FROM PASSION

Registering your business involves providing basic information about your business, such as the legal structure, business name, address, and owner information. You'll also need to obtain any necessary licenses and permits, such as a business license or zoning permit.

In addition to registering your business, it's important to obtain any necessary insurance to protect your business from risks such as liability, property damage, and business interruption. Depending on your industry and location, you may be required to carry certain types of insurance, such as workers' compensation insurance or professional liability insurance.

Overall, choosing a legal structure and registering your business can be a complex process with important legal and financial implications. It's important to do your research and consult with professionals to ensure that you choose the structure that best suits your business's needs and comply with all requirements. By taking the time to get this right, you'll be laying a solid foundation for your business's success.

Choosing a legal structure and registering your business is a critical step in the process of starting and running a business. It not only defines the legal framework within which your business will operate, but also affects taxation, liability, and funding options. As such, it is important to make informed decisions about your legal structure and registration.

There are several legal structures to choose from, including sole proprietorship, partnership, limited liability company (LLC), corporation, and cooperative. Each structure has its advantages and disadvantages, and the right choice depends on factors such as the size and scope of your business, your liability preferences, and tax considerations.

❖ Sole Proprietorship

A sole proprietorship is the simplest and most common legal structure for small businesses. As the name suggests, it is owned and operated by a single person. One advantage of a sole proprietorship is that it is easy and inexpensive to set up, as it requires no formal legal documents or filings. Additionally, the owner has complete control over the business and all profits are considered personal income and taxed accordingly.

However, a major disadvantage of a sole proprietorship is that the owner is personally liable for all debts and obligations of the business, meaning that personal assets may be at risk in the event of legal action or financial problems.

❖ Partnership

A partnership is a legal structure in which two or more people share ownership of a business. There are two types of partnerships: general partnerships and limited partnerships. In a general partnership, each partner is equally responsible for the debts and obligations of the business. In a limited partnership, there is at least one general partner who is responsible for the debts and obligations, while the other partners have limited liability.

One advantage of a partnership is that it allows for the sharing of responsibilities and resources, as well as the pooling of different skills and expertise. Additionally, partnerships are relatively easy and inexpensive to set up and can benefit from lower tax rates.

However, partnerships also have their drawbacks. Partnerships are subject to disagreements and conflicts between partners, which can negatively impact the business. Additionally, each partner is liable for the actions of the others, meaning that personal assets may be at risk in the event of legal action or financial problems.

❖ Limited Liability Company (LLC)

A limited liability company (LLC) is a legal structure that combines the liability protection of a corporation with the tax benefits of a partnership. This means that the owners (known as members) are not personally liable for the debts and obligations of the business. Additionally, an LLC can choose to be taxed as a sole proprietorship, partnership, S corporation, or C corporation.

One advantage of an LLC is that it provides liability protection for the owners, meaning that personal assets are not at risk in the event of legal action or financial problems. Additionally, an LLC is flexible in terms of management and can be owned and operated by a single member or multiple members.

However, an LLC also has its drawbacks. It can be more complex and expensive to set up than a sole proprietorship or partnership and may require the assistance of a lawyer or accountant. Additionally, an LLC is subject to state regulations, which can vary depending on the state in which it is registered.

❖ Corporation

PROFITS FROM PASSION

A corporation is a legal structure that is owned by shareholders and managed by a board of directors. A corporation is considered a separate legal entity from its owners, meaning that the corporation is liable for its debts and obligations. Additionally, shareholders are only liable for the amount of their investment in the corporation.

One advantage of a corporation is that it provides the greatest liability protection for the owners, meaning that personal assets are not at risk in the event of legal action or financial problems. Additionally, corporations can issue stocks and raise capital from investors.

SETTING UP YOUR WORKSPACE AND EQUIPMENT

Setting up your workspace and equipment is crucial for any business, regardless of the industry. Having a functional workspace and the right equipment can increase productivity and efficiency, as well as improve the overall work environment. In this article, we will explore the key factors to consider when setting up your workspace and equipment, along with some examples and tips for success.

- Designing your workspace

The first step in setting up your workspace is designing the layout. The layout of your workspace should be functional, efficient, and conducive to the type of work you will be doing. This means considering factors such as the size and shape of the space, the furniture and equipment needed, and the flow of traffic within the space.

For example, if you are setting up a home office, you will need to consider the size of the room and the placement of furniture and equipment. You may also want to consider factors such as lighting and soundproofing to create a comfortable and productive work environment.

- Choosing the right equipment

Once you have designed your workspace, the next step is to choose the right equipment. This includes things such as computers, printers, scanners, and other office equipment. When choosing equipment, you should consider factors such as the size and functionality of the equipment, as well as your budget. For example, if you are setting up a graphic design studio, you will need to invest in high-quality computers, monitors, and graphic tablets. On the other hand, if you are setting up a home-based accounting business, you may only need a basic computer and printer.

- Investing in quality furniture

Investing in quality furniture is also important for setting up your workspace. This includes desks, chairs, and other ergonomic equipment. The right furniture can not only improve your posture and reduce the risk of injury, but it can also improve your overall productivity and efficiency.

For example, if you are setting up a law office, you may want to invest in high-quality chairs and desks that provide proper support and comfort during long periods of sitting. Alternatively, if you are setting up a yoga studio, you may want to invest in yoga mats, blocks, and other equipment that will enhance the practice.

- Considering your storage needs

Storage is also an important factor to consider when setting up your workspace. Depending on the type of business you are setting up, you may need to invest in filing cabinets, shelves, or other storage solutions.

For example, if you are setting up a photography studio, you will need to invest in storage solutions for your cameras, lenses, and other equipment. Alternatively, if you are setting up a home-based catering business, you may need to invest in storage solutions for your ingredients and supplies.

- Enhancing your workspace with decor

Finally, enhancing your workspace with decor can help create a comfortable and inspiring work environment. This includes things such as artwork, plants, and other decorative items that reflect your brand and personality.

For example, if you are setting up a home-based graphic design business, you may want to decorate your workspace with artwork that reflects your design style. Alternatively, if you are setting up a home-based massage therapy business, you may want to decorate your workspace with calming colors and plants to create a relaxing environment.

In conclusion, setting up your workspace and equipment is a crucial step in starting a business. By designing a functional workspace, investing in quality equipment and furniture, considering your storage needs, and enhancing your workspace with decor, you can create a comfortable and productive work environment that sets you up for success.

UNDERSTANDING TAX REQUIREMENTS AND OBLIGATIONS

As an entrepreneur, understanding tax requirements and obligations is crucial for the success and sustainability of your business. Taxes are a necessary part of running a business and failing to comply with tax regulations can result in legal and financial consequences. In this article, we will discuss the different types of taxes that businesses are required to pay, how to register for them and some tips on how to stay compliant.

1. Types of Business Taxes

There are several types of taxes that businesses are required to pay. Here are some of the most common ones:

- ✓ Income Tax: This is a tax on the profits earned by your business. Businesses are required to pay income tax on their net income, which is calculated by subtracting business expenses from revenues.
- ✓ Sales Tax: This is a tax on the sale of goods and services. Depending on the state, sales tax rates may vary, and some products and services may be exempt from sales tax.
- ✓ Payroll Tax: This is a tax on wages and salaries paid to employees. As an employer, you are required to withhold payroll taxes from your employees' paychecks and remit them to the government on their behalf.

PROFITS FROM PASSION

✓ Property Tax: This is a tax on real estate and personal property owned by your business. The amount of property tax you pay is based on the assessed value of your property.

2. Registering for Business Taxes

Once you have identified the types of taxes that apply to your business, the next step is to register for them. Here's how:

Obtain an Employer Identification Number (EIN): An EIN is a unique identifier assigned to your business by the IRS. You can apply for an EIN online through the IRS website.

✓ Register with your State: Most states require businesses to register for sales and use tax, payroll tax, and other taxes. You can register with your state's tax agency online or by mail.

✓ Obtain a Business License: Depending on the type of business you have, you may need to obtain a business license from your local government. The requirements for obtaining a license vary depending on the location of your business.

Tips for Staying Compliant with Tax Regulations

Here are some tips to help you stay compliant with tax regulations:

✓ Keep Accurate Records: Maintaining accurate records of your income and expenses is crucial for calculating your taxes accurately. Use accounting software or hire a bookkeeper to help you keep track of your finances.

✓ Remit Taxes on Time: Make sure to remit your taxes on time to avoid penalties and interest charges. Set up a reminder system to ensure that you don't miss any deadlines.

✓ Seek Professional Help: If you're unsure about your tax obligations, seek help from a tax professional. They can guide how to comply with tax regulations and help you avoid potential legal and financial consequences.

Conclusion

Understanding tax requirements and obligations is an essential part of running a successful business. By identifying the types of taxes that apply to your business, registering for them, and staying compliant with tax regulations, you can avoid legal and financial consequences and focus on growing your business. Remember to keep accurate records, remit taxes on time, and seek professional help if you're unsure about your tax obligations.

HIRING EMPLOYEES AND/OR CONTRACTORS

Hiring employees or contractors is a crucial step for any business owner looking to grow their operations. As the workload increases, it becomes impossible to handle everything alone, and hiring staff becomes necessary. However, this process can be overwhelming, especially for first-time business owners. Understanding the difference between employees and contractors, and the legal requirements for each, is crucial to avoid any legal complications down the line.

Employees are individuals who work for a company on a full-time, part-time, or temporary basis, under an employment contract. The employment contract typically outlines the terms of the job, including the job description, pay, hours of work, benefits, and other details. Employees are entitled to certain protections under federal and state labor laws, including minimum wage, overtime pay, and workers' compensation.

On the other hand, contractors, also known as freelancers or independent contractors, work for a company on a project-by-project basis. They are typically hired to perform a specific task or project, and their payment is often based on the project's completion. Contractors are not considered employees and are not entitled to the same legal protections as employees. Instead, they are responsible for paying their taxes, purchasing their equipment, and managing their schedules.

When hiring employees, there are several legal requirements that business owners must meet. First, they must obtain an employer identification number (EIN) from the Internal Revenue Service (IRS). This number is used to identify the business entity for tax purposes. Second, they must complete the necessary paperwork for each employee, including a Form W-4, which specifies the employee's withholding allowances, and a Form I-9, which verifies the employee's eligibility to work in the United States.

In addition to these requirements, business owners must also comply with federal and state labor laws. These laws dictate various aspects of employment, including minimum wage requirements, overtime pay, and workers' compensation. Business owners must also withhold taxes from employee paychecks, including federal income tax, Social Security tax, and Medicare tax.

When hiring contractors, the process is slightly different. Contractors are typically responsible for their taxes and are not considered employees for tax purposes. However, business owners must still ensure that the contractor is legally authorized to work in the United States and that they are not misclassified as an employee. Misclassifying a contractor as an employee can result in legal consequences, including fines and penalties.

It's important to note that the legal requirements for hiring employees and contractors vary by state and industry. Therefore, it's crucial to consult with an experienced attorney or accountant to ensure that your business complies with all relevant laws and regulations.

In addition to legal requirements, there are several practical considerations when hiring employees or contractors. These include determining the job responsibilities, creating job descriptions, interviewing candidates, and setting compensation and benefits packages.

When determining job responsibilities, it's essential to consider the skills and experience required for the job, as well as any necessary certifications or licenses. Creating a clear and concise job description will help attract the right candidates and set expectations for the role.

Interviewing candidates is a crucial step in the hiring process. It's essential to ask open-ended questions that allow candidates to showcase their skills and experience. Additionally, it's important to conduct background checks and verify the candidate's references to ensure that they are qualified for the job.

Setting compensation and benefits packages can be a complex process. It's essential to consider industry standards and the cost of living in your area when determining pay. Additionally, offering benefits, such as health insurance and retirement plans, can be a valuable tool for attracting and retaining top talent.

In summary, hiring employees or contractors is a crucial step in growing a business. Business owners must understand the legal requirements for each and take practical considerations into account when making hiring decisions.

CHAPTER FIVE
LAUNCHING AND GROWING YOUR BUSINESS
LAUNCHING YOUR BUSINESS WITH A BANG

Launching a business can be both exciting and nerve-wracking. It's the culmination of months, or even years, of hard work and planning. However, the success of your launch can have a significant impact on the future of your business. A successful launch can help create buzz, generate interest, and attract potential customers. On the other hand, a lackluster launch can result in a slow start, missed opportunities, and a difficult road ahead. In this article, we'll discuss how to launch your business with a bang, with examples and strategies that can help make your launch a success.

A. Plan Ahead

A successful launch requires careful planning and preparation. One of the first steps is to set a launch date and start planning well in advance. Consider the following questions:

- What is the purpose of your launch?
- What goals do you hope to achieve?
- Who is your target audience?
- What marketing and promotional strategies will you use?
- What resources will you need?
- Who will be involved in the launch?

Answering these questions will help you develop a clear launch plan and ensure that everyone involved is on the same page.

B. Generate Buzz

PROFITS FROM PASSION

Before your launch, it's important to create buzz and generate interest in your business. Here are a few strategies that can help:

- Teasers: Create teasers and sneak peeks of your product or service. This can include images, videos, or other content that gives potential customers a taste of what's to come.
- Social Media: Use social media platforms like Twitter, Facebook, and Instagram to create buzz and generate interest. Consider running a social media contest or giveaway to encourage engagement.
- Influencers: Consider partnering with influencers in your industry or niche to help promote your launch. Influencers can help you reach a larger audience and build credibility with potential customers.
- Media Coverage: Reach out to journalists and media outlets to generate media coverage for your launch. This can include press releases, media pitches, or interviews.

C. Host a Launch Event

Hosting a launch event can be a great way to generate buzz, create excitement, and attract potential customers. Here are a few tips for hosting a successful launch event:

- Venue: Choose a venue that is appropriate for your audience and the size of your event. This could be a conference room, a restaurant, or even a public space.
- Invitations: Send out invitations well in advance of your event. Consider using a platform like Eventbrite to manage RSVPs and track attendance.

PROFITS FROM PASSION

- Speakers: Consider inviting guest speakers or experts in your industry to speak at your event. This can help build credibility and provide valuable insights for your audience.
- Demos: If possible, provide demos or hands-on experiences of your product or service. This can help potential customers understand your offering and build excitement.
- Giveaways: Consider offering giveaways or prizes at your event. This can include branded merchandise, gift cards, or other incentives to encourage attendance and engagement.

D. Use Paid Advertising

Paid advertising can be an effective way to reach a larger audience and generate interest in your launch. Consider the following options:

- Google Ads: Use Google Ads to target potential customers who are searching for keywords related to your business. This can help drive traffic to your website and increase awareness.
- Social Media Ads: Use social media ads to target potential customers on platforms like Facebook, Instagram, and Twitter. This can help build brand awareness and generate leads.
- Display Ads: Use display ads on websites and blogs related to your industry or niche. This can help reach a wider audience and generate interest in your launch.

E. Leverage Email Marketing

Email marketing can be a powerful tool for launching your business. Here are a few tips to help you get started:

PROFITS FROM PASSION

Build Your List: Build a list of subscribers

Building a list of subscribers is an important aspect of marketing for any business, and it is especially crucial when launching a new venture. Your email list is essentially a database of contacts who have expressed interest in your business and have permitted you to contact them via email.

Here are a few tips for building your email list:

- ❖ Offer a valuable incentive: Offer an incentive, such as a free e-book or discount code, in exchange for visitors subscribing to your email list. This will encourage them to sign up and provide their email address.
- ❖ Include opt-in forms on your website: Make it easy for visitors to subscribe to your email list by including opt-in forms on your website. Place them in prominent locations, such as in the header or footer of your website, or as a pop-up when someone visits your site.
- ❖ Use social media: Use your social media channels to promote your email list and encourage followers to sign up. Share a link to your opt-in form and highlight the benefits of subscribing.
- ❖ Host a contest or giveaway: Host a contest or giveaway and require entrants to subscribe to your email list to participate. This is a great way to not only build your email list but also increase engagement and brand awareness.

Once you have built your email list, it's important to use it effectively. Here are some tips for leveraging email marketing to launch your business:

PROFITS FROM PASSION

❖ Craft engaging subject lines: Your subject line is the first thing recipients will see, so make it engaging and attention-grabbing. Avoid using spammy language or making false promises.

❖ Provide valuable content: Provide your subscribers with valuable content that is relevant to their interests. This will help establish your brand as a trusted source of information and keep subscribers engaged.

❖ Segment your list: Segmenting your email list allows you to send targeted messages to specific groups of subscribers based on their interests or behaviors. This can increase the effectiveness of your email campaigns and help prevent subscribers from becoming disengaged.

❖ Use a clear call-to-action: Include a clear call-to-action in your emails, such as encouraging subscribers to visit your website, make a purchase, or sign up for a free trial. Make it easy for them to take action by including clear links and buttons.

❖ Test and optimize: Test different elements of your email campaigns, such as subject lines, content, and calls to action, to see what resonates best with your audience. Use this information to optimize future campaigns for better results.

Overall, building an email list and leveraging email marketing can be a powerful tool for launching your business and building a strong relationship with your audience. By providing valuable content and optimizing your campaigns, you can increase engagement, drive conversions, and ultimately achieve success.

SCALING UP YOUR BUSINESS OVER TIME

Scaling up a business is a natural progression for most entrepreneurs. As your business grows, you will need to make changes to your operations, staff, and finances. Here are some tips to help you scale your business successfully:

a) Develop a Clear Growth Strategy

To scale your business, you need to have a clear understanding of your goals, target market, and competition. Your growth strategy should outline how you plan to increase revenue, expand your customer base, and develop new products or services.

For example, if you own a restaurant, your growth strategy may include opening new locations, expanding your menu, and investing in marketing to attract new customers.

b) Focus on Customer Retention

Acquiring new customers is important, but retaining existing customers is even more crucial for scaling up your business. A study by Bain & Company found that increasing customer retention rates by just 5% can increase profits by up to 95%.

To retain your customers, you need to provide them with a positive experience every time they interact with your business. This includes offering exceptional customer service, personalized communication, and loyalty programs.

c) Streamline Your Operations

PROFITS FROM PASSION

As your business grows, you will need to streamline your operations to improve efficiency and reduce costs. This may involve automating certain tasks, outsourcing non-core functions, and implementing new technology.

For example, if you run an e-commerce business, you may need to invest in a warehouse management system to help you manage inventory and orders more effectively.

d) Hire the Right People

Scaling up your business requires a team of talented and dedicated employees. You need to hire the right people who share your vision and are committed to helping your business grow.

When hiring, look for candidates with the right skills, experience, and attitude. You should also invest in employee training and development to ensure your team has the knowledge and skills they need to support your business as it grows.

e) Manage Your Finances Carefully

As your business grows, your finances will become more complex. You need to manage your cash flow carefully, monitor your expenses, and plan for growth.

This may involve investing in new equipment, hiring additional staff, or expanding your marketing budget. You should also consider working with a financial advisor to help you manage your finances effectively.

f) Stay Agile and Flexible

Scaling up your business requires a willingness to adapt to change and embrace new opportunities. You need to be agile and flexible in your approach, and willing to pivot if something isn't working.

For example, if you own a retail store and notice that online sales are growing faster than in-store sales, you may need to shift your focus and invest more in your online presence.

g) Measure Your Progress

To know if you're on track to achieving your growth goals, you need to measure your progress regularly. This may involve tracking key performance indicators (KPIs) such as revenue, customer retention rates, and employee satisfaction.

By tracking your progress, you can identify areas where you need to improve and make adjustments to your strategy as needed.

In conclusion, scaling up your business takes time, effort, and careful planning. By following these tips, you can successfully grow your business and take it to the next level.

DEVELOPING A LOYAL CUSTOMER BASE

Developing a loyal customer base is a critical component of any successful business. A loyal customer base is a group of customers who consistently choose your business over your competitors, and who are willing to promote your products or services to others. These customers are essential to the long-term success and growth of your business.

So, how can you develop a loyal customer base? Here are some strategies to consider:

PROFITS FROM PASSION

✓ Provide Excellent Customer Service:

One of the most important things you can do to develop a loyal customer base is to provide excellent customer service. Customers are more likely to return to your business if they have a positive experience. Make sure your employees are trained to handle customer complaints and inquiries with empathy and efficiency. Respond promptly to customer inquiries, and go above and beyond to resolve any issues they may have.

✓ Offer Incentives:

Offering incentives to customers can be a powerful way to develop a loyal customer base. For example, you could offer discounts to customers who refer their friends to your business, or you could offer loyalty rewards programs to encourage customers to return to your business. Consider what incentives are most likely to appeal to your target audience and tailor your approach accordingly.

✓ Build a Strong Online Presence:

In today's digital age, it's more important than ever to build a strong online presence. This includes having a well-designed website, active social media accounts, and positive online reviews. Make sure your website is user-friendly and easy to navigate, and that it provides customers with all the information they need to make an informed decision about your products or services. Use social media to engage with your customers and build relationships with them. Encourage satisfied customers to leave positive reviews on sites like Yelp or Google Reviews.

✓ Personalize Your Marketing:

PROFITS FROM PASSION

Personalized marketing can be a powerful way to develop a loyal customer base. By tailoring your marketing efforts to the individual preferences and needs of your customers, you can make them feel valued and appreciated. This could include sending personalized emails or targeted social media ads based on customers' previous purchases or browsing history.

✓ Stay in Touch:

Staying in touch with your customers is critical to developing a loyal customer base. This could include sending regular newsletters or emails with updates about your business, new products or services, or special promotions. You could also use social media to keep your customers informed about what's going on with your business. By staying top-of-mind with your customers, you can build strong relationships that keep them coming back.

✓ Provide Value:

Ultimately, the key to developing a loyal customer base is to provide value. This means offering high-quality products or services at a fair price and going above and beyond to meet the needs of your customers. If your customers feel that they are getting good value for their money, they are more likely to return to your business and recommend it to others.

In conclusion, developing a loyal customer base is critical to the long-term success and growth of any business. By providing excellent customer service, offering incentives, building a strong online presence, personalizing your marketing, staying in touch, and providing value, you can build strong relationships with your customers that keep them coming back.

MEASURING YOUR BUSINESS SUCCESS AND MAKING ADJUSTMENTS

As an entrepreneur, it is essential to measure your business success and make adjustments to ensure that your business is on the right track. There are many metrics that you can use to measure your business success, such as revenue, profit margin, customer satisfaction, and employee engagement. In this article, we will explore these metrics in more detail and provide examples of how you can measure and make adjustments to improve your business's success.

❖ Revenue

Revenue is the total amount of money that your business generates from sales of goods or services. Revenue is a crucial metric because it is a measure of your business's ability to generate income. You can measure your revenue by tracking your sales on a daily, weekly, monthly, or annual basis. Revenue can be broken down further into different revenue streams, such as sales from specific products or services.

Example: Suppose you own a restaurant that generates revenue from food and beverage sales. You can measure your revenue by tracking your sales daily and identifying which menu items are most popular among customers. If you find that certain menu items are not selling well, you can adjust your menu and marketing strategies to improve sales.

❖ Profit Margin

PROFITS FROM PASSION

Profit margin is the amount of money your business earns after deducting expenses from revenue. Profit margin is an important metric because it measures your business's profitability. You can measure your profit margin by calculating your net income divided by your total revenue. Profit margin can be improved by increasing revenue or decreasing expenses.

Example: Suppose you own an e-commerce business that sells handmade jewelry. You can measure your profit margin by calculating your net income divided by your total revenue. If you find that your profit margin is low, you can adjust your pricing strategy or reduce your overhead expenses to increase profitability.

❖ Customer Satisfaction

Customer satisfaction is the measure of how happy your customers are with your products or services. Customer satisfaction is crucial because satisfied customers are more likely to return and recommend your business to others. You can measure customer satisfaction through surveys, feedback forms, and online reviews.

Example: Suppose you own a beauty salon that provides hair and makeup services. You can measure customer satisfaction by sending out surveys to customers after their appointments to gather feedback on their experience. If you find that customers are not satisfied with certain aspects of your services, you can make adjustments to improve customer satisfaction.

❖ Employee Engagement

PROFITS FROM PASSION

Employee engagement is the measure of how committed and motivated your employees are to their work. Employee engagement is important because engaged employees are more productive and provide better customer service. You can measure employee engagement through surveys and feedback forms.

Example: Suppose you own a marketing agency that provides digital marketing services. You can measure employee engagement by sending out surveys to employees to gather feedback on their job satisfaction and motivation. If you find that employees are not engaged, you can make adjustments to improve employee morale and motivation.

❖ Making Adjustments

Once you have measured your business success, you can make adjustments to improve your metrics. Making adjustments can involve changing your business strategies, improving your products or services, or investing in new technology. It is important to monitor your metrics over time to see if your adjustments are having a positive impact on your business.

Example: Suppose you own a fitness studio that offers group fitness classes. You notice that attendance for certain classes is low. You can make adjustments by offering promotions for those classes, changing the class schedule, or improving the class content. By monitoring attendance after making adjustments, you can see if your changes have had a positive impact on your business's success.

PROFITS FROM PASSION

In conclusion, measuring your business success is essential for ensuring that your business is on the right track. By tracking metrics such as revenue, profit margin, customer satisfaction, and employee engagement, you can identify areas for improvement and make adjustments to improve your business's success. With dedication and hard work, you can build a thriving business.